Bird's Eye

⬦ Q U I L T ⬦

by

Judy Knoechel

A Quilt in a Day® Publication

To Susan *A special thanks*

To Marcia *Our long distance runner and my favorite over-achiever*

To Lucina *Our fifth sister*

To Mackie *Because she is always there for me*

And to the Dream Team *Matt, Orion, Richard, Robert and Grant*

Published by Quilt in a Day, Inc.

1955 Diamond Street, San Marcos, CA 92069

Copyright © 1993 by Judy Knoechel

ISBN   0-922705-40-2

Editor Eleanor Burns

Art Direction Merritt Voigtlander

Desktop Publishing Susan Sells

Photography Wayne Norton

Photostylist Marian Buzbee

Table of Contents

Introduction

For many years I have considered myself a backstage person at Quilt in a Day. I have been happily involved with the wholesale distribution and would prefer to remain anonymous, except for the inescapable fact that I am related to Eleanor Burns and Patricia Knoechel. To the multitude of people who thread their way through our building each year, I am proudly introduced as Eleanor's sister. Their first reaction is to question if I also am a quilter. My standard reply has been, "No, actually I am a weaver and help to balance our range of accomplishments. My sisters have my rugs in their homes and I have their quilts in mine."

I enjoyed watching people cut and sew quilts. I especially enjoyed seeing the completed projects and listening to the stories that went with them, but I didn't particularly want to try any pattern more complicated than the Log Cabin or Irish Chain.

One day Mackie hung a bargello quilt on the wall of the classroom and I was intrigued with the pattern. I looked at it through weaver's eyes. It looked like something I could duplicate on my loom. The quilt inspired me to sign up for the class. And like the sentiment on the t-shirt, I began to believe in miracles: I finished my quilt. After that I signed up to take other classes and was constantly impressed with the unique assembly-line techniques that produced each pattern. Like my sisters, I wanted to take a quilt pattern, break it down to its roots and invent a system of steps to construct it.

When I looked at the traditional quilt patterns that Eleanor studies for inspiration, I was overwhelmed. When I looked in my weaving books for ideas, I found myself in familiar territory. It was a simple matter to take the Bird's Eye weaving draft and convert it to block shapes on draft paper. The humble little diamond design grew into all the ideas and techniques contained within the pages of this book.

I invite you to work along step by step with me, but beware: who knows what latent creativity you might awaken!

Planning Your Quilt

Setting Choice

The Yardage and Cutting Charts give information for a Classic setting of the Bird's Eye in which the blocks are framed with the same background fabric. The other choice is setting the blocks together with Lattice and Cornerstones. If you prefer the Lattice and Cornerstone setting, choose fabrics to compliment the blocks.

Finishing

Finish the quilt with either the Machine Quilting and Binding instructions or the easier method of a Quick Turn and Tie.

Use a thin bonded batting for Machine Quilting and a thick bonded batting for a tied quilt.

Sample Block

Fabric

Choose 100% cotton fabrics of the same weight and at least 42" wide. Do not use polyester blends.

Color Selection

The Bird's Eye pattern has five fabrics in the block. Choose two or three or even four main colors.

The background color, **1**, can be a light or a dark or a medium value. The important consideration is showing contrast between fabrics **1** and **2**. Fabric **2** should always be a strong color since it frames the outline of the pattern. The color and value of fabric **3** should be less dominant. Other than that, this quilt pattern offers a wide range of color selection.

In order to show good contrast, choose prints of various small scales in different values. Avoid directional prints. Do not use a large floral in the block, but you may want to incorporate one in a border. Do not plan "fussy cuts" because the assembly-line construction does not lend itself to selecting and cutting specific motifs.

The distinct geometric line of this quilt is striking in southwest fabrics. Soft and delicate colors are perfect for a baby quilt. A black background sets off bold, jewel colors.

Cut ¾" strips of fabrics **1**, **2**, **3**, **4**, and **5** for the Fabric Choices for the Classic Bird's Eye setting.

For the Lattice and Cornerstone setting, also use Fabrics **6** and **7**.

Cut squares and strips to correspond with the block parts.

Use a glue stick to paste them in place.

Lattice & Cornerstones Setting Only

1	2	3	4	5	6	7

1 or 7	1 or 6							1 or 7
			1	2	1			
	1	1	2	3	2	1	1	
		2	3	4	3	2		
1 or 6	2	3	4	5	4	3	2	1 or 6
		2	3	4	3	2		
	1	1	2	3	2	1	1	
			1	2	1			
1 or 7	1 or 6							1 or 7

Supplies

100% cotton fabric, 44" wide

Sewing machine with ¼" presser foot

All purpose neutral or grey thread

Large rotary cutter with sharp blade

Gridded cutting mat 18" x 24"

6" x 6" Plexiglass ruler

6" x 24" Plexiglass ruler

6" x 12" Plexiglass ruler

12 ½" Square Up ruler

Serger (optional)

Magnetic seam guide

Extra long quilter's pins

Stiletto

Scissors

Ironing board

Steam iron

Machine quilting finish

    Invisible thread

    Walking foot

    1" Safety pins and "Kwik Klip" tool

    Thin batting

Quick turn finish

    Curved needle

    Embroidery floss for tying

    Thick batting

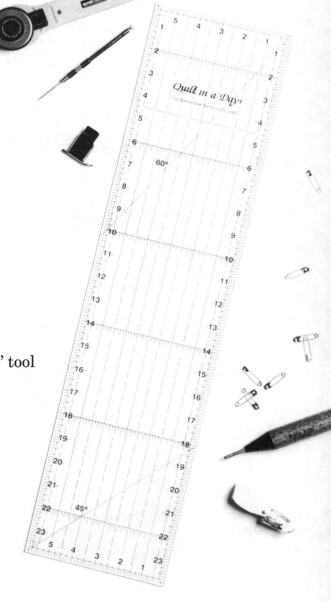

Cutting Straight Strips

Use a large industrial size rotary cutter with a sharp blade and a 6" x 24" plexiglass ruler on a gridded cutting mat.

1. Make a nick on the selvage edge, and tear your fabric from selvage to selvage to put the fabric on the straight of the grain.

2. Fold the fabric in half, matching the torn straight edge thread to thread.

3. With the fold of the fabric at the bottom, line up the torn edge of fabric on the gridded cutting mat with the left edge extended slightly to the left of zero. Reverse this procedure if you are left-handed.

4. Line up the 6" x 24" ruler on zero. Spread the fingers of your left hand to hold the ruler firmly. With the rotary cutter in your right hand, begin cutting with the blade off the fabric on the mat. Put all your strength into the rotary cutter as you cut away from you, and trim the torn, ragged edge.

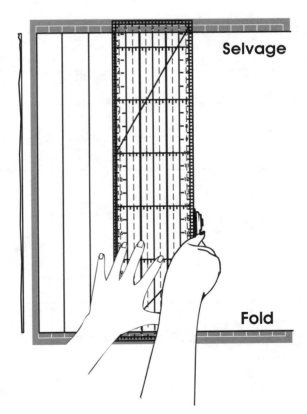

Selvage

Fold

5. Lift, and move the ruler over until it lines up with the desired strip width on the grid and cut. Accuracy is important.

6. Open the first strip to see if it is straight. Check periodically. Make a straightening cut when necessary.

Yardage and Cutting Charts
Baby Quilt

9 Blocks - 3 x 3   Approximate size: 40" x 40"
Cut all strips selvage to selvage.

Classic

☐ Fabric 1

Background	1¼ yds.	Cut (2) 5" strips
		(2) 3½" strips
		(10) 2" strips

■ Fabric 2

	⅔ yd.	Cut (7) 2" strips

■ Fabric 3

	½ yd.	Cut (5) 2" strips

■ Fabric 4

	⅜ yd.	Cut (3) 2" strips

■ Fabric 5

	⅛ yd.	Cut (1) 2" strip

■ Border

	⅔ yd.	Cut (4) 3½" strips

Backing

	1¼ yds.

Batting

	45" x 45"

Binding for Machine Quilted Finish Only

½ yd.	Cut (4) 3" strips

Lattice and Cornerstones

☐ Fabric 1

Background	⅞ yd.	Cut (2) 5" strips
		(2) 3½ strips
		(2) 2" strips

■ Fabric 2

	⅔ yd.	Cut (7) 2" strips

■ Fabric 3

	½ yd.	Cut (5) 2" strips

■ Fabric 4

	⅜ yd.	Cut (3) 2" strips

■ Fabric 5

	⅛ yd.	Cut (1) 2" strip

■ Lattice

	⅔ yd.	Cut (8) 2"strips

■ Cornerstones

	⅛ yd.	Cut (1) 2" strip

■ Border

	⅔ yd.	Cut (4) 3½" strips

Backing

	1¼ yds.

Batting

	45" x 45"

Binding for Machine Quilted Finish Only

½ yd.	Cut (4) 3" strips

Lap Quilt

18 Blocks - 3 x 6   Approximate size: 40" x 74"
Cut all strips selvage to selvage.

Classic

☐ **Fabric 1**		
Background	2¼ yds.	Cut (4) 5" strips
		(4) 3½" strips
		(19) 2" strips
■ **Fabric 2**		
	⅞ yd.	Cut (12) 2" strips
■ **Fabric 3**		
	⅔ yd.	Cut (8) 2" strips
■ **Fabric 4**		
	⅜ yd.	Cut (4) 2" strips
■ **Fabric 5**		
	⅛ yd.	Cut (1) 2" strip
■ **Border**		
	¾ yd.	Cut (6) 3½" strips
Backing		
	2¼ yds.	
Batting		
	45" x 80"	
Binding for Machine Quilted Finish Only		
	¾ yd.	Cut (6) 3" strips

Lattice and Cornerstones

☐ **Fabric 1**		
Background	1½ yds.	Cut (4) 5" strips
		(4) 3½" strips
		(4) 2" strips
■ **Fabric 2**		
	⅞ yd.	Cut (12) 2" strips
■ **Fabric 3**		
	⅔ yd.	Cut (8) 2" strips
■ **Fabric 4**		
	⅜ yd.	Cut (4) 2" strips
■ **Fabric 5**		
	⅛ yd.	Cut (1) 2" strip
■ **Lattice**		
	1⅛ yds.	Cut (15) 2" strips
■ **Cornerstones**		
	¼ yd.	Cut (2) 2" strips
■ **Border**		
	¾ yd.	Cut (6) 3½ strips
Backing		
	2¼ yds.	
Batting		
	45" x 80"	
Binding for Machine Quilted Finish Only		
	¾ yd.	Cut (6) 3" strips

Twin Quilt

18 Blocks - 3 x 6   Approximate size: 60" x 94"
Cut all strips selvage to selvage.

Classic

☐ **Fabric 1**		
Background	2¼ yds.	Cut (4) 5" strips
		(4) 3½" strips
		(19) 2" strips
■ **Fabric 2**		
	⅞ yd.	Cut (12) 2" strips
■ **Fabric 3**		
	⅔ yd.	Cut (8) 2" strips
■ **Fabric 4**		
	⅜ yd.	Cut (4) 2" strips
■ **Fabric 5**		
	⅛ yd.	Cut (1) 2" strip
■ **First Border**		
	⅞ yd.	Cut (6) 4" strips
■ **Second Border**		
	1¼ yds.	Cut (7) 5" strips
■ **Third Border**		
	1⅝ yds.	Cut (8) 6" strips
Backing		
	6 yds.	Cut (2) 3 yds. pieces
Batting		
	70" x 108"	
Binding for Machine Quilted Finish Only		
	1 yd.	Cut (8) 3" strips

Lattice and Cornertones

☐ **Fabric 1**		
Background	1½ yds.	Cut (4) 5" strips
		(4) 3½" strips
		(4) 2" strips
■ **Fabric 2**		
	⅞ yd.	Cut (12) 2" strips
■ **Fabric 3**		
	⅔ yd.	Cut (8) 2" strips
■ **Fabric 4**		
	⅜ yd.	Cut (4) 2" strips
■ **Fabric 5**		
	⅛ yd.	Cut (1) 2" strip
■ **Lattice**		
	1⅛ yds.	Cut (15) 2" strips
■ **Cornerstones**		
	¼ yd.	Cut (2) 2" strips
■ **First Border**		
	⅞ yd.	Cut (6) 4" strips
■ **Second Border**		
	1¼ yds.	Cut (7) 5" strips
■ **Third Border**		
	1⅝ yds.	Cut (8) 6" strips
Backing		
	6 yds.	Cut (2) 3 yds. pieces
Batting		
	70" x 108"	
Binding for Machine Quilted Finish Only		
	1 yd.	Cut (8) 3" strips

Double Quilt

35 Blocks - 5 x 7   Approximate size: 75" x 98"
Cut all strips selvage to selvage.

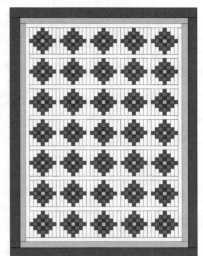

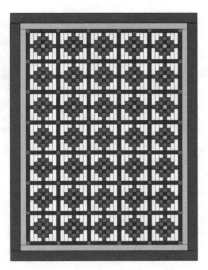

Classic

☐ **Fabric 1**		
Background	4⅛ yds.	Cut (8) 5" strips
		(8) 3½" strips
		(34) 2" strips
■ **Fabric 2**		
	1⅝ yds.	Cut (24) 2" strips
■ **Fabric 3**		
	1⅛ yds.	Cut (16) 2" strips
■ **Fabric 4**		
	⅔ yd.	Cut (8) 2" strips
■ **Fabric 5**		
	¼ yd.	Cut (2) 2" strips
■ **First Border**		
	1⅛ yds.	Cut (8) 4" strips
■ **Second Border**		
	1¾ yds.	Cut (9) 6" strips
Backing		
	6 yds.	Cut (2) 3 yds. pieces
Batting		
	90" x 108"	
Binding for Machine Quilted Finish Only		
	1 yd.	Cut (9) 3" strips

Lattice and Cornerstones

☐ **Fabric 1**		
Background	2⅝ yds.	Cut (8) 5" strips
		(8) 3½" strips
		(8) 2" strips
■ **Fabric 2**		
	1⅝ yds.	Cut (24) 2" strips
■ **Fabric 3**		
	1⅛ yds.	Cut (16) 2" strips
■ **Fabric 4**		
	⅔ yd.	Cut (8) 2" strips
■ **Fabric 5**		
	¼ yd.	Cut (2) 2" strips
■ **Lattice**		
	1¾ yds.	Cut (28) 2" strips
■ **Cornerstones**		
	⅓ yd.	Cut (3) 2" strips
■ **First Border**		
	1⅛ yds.	Cut (8) 4" strips
■ **Second Border**		
	1¾ yds.	Cut (9) 6" strips
Backing		
	6 yds.	Cut (2) 3 yds. pieces
Batting		
	90" x 108"	
Binding for Machine Quilted Finish Only		
	1 yd.	Cut (9) 3" strips

Queen Quilt

35 Blocks - 5 x 7   Approximate size: 84" x 107"
Cut all strips selvage to selvage.

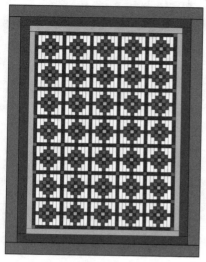

Classic

☐ **Fabric 1**			
Background	4⅛ yds.		Cut (8) 5" strips
			(8) 3½" strips
			(34) 2" strips
■ **Fabric 2**			
	1⅝ yds.		Cut (24) 2" strips
■ **Fabric 3**			
	1⅛ yds.		Cut (16) 2" strips
■ **Fabric 4**			
	⅔ yd.		Cut (8) 2" strips
■ **Fabric 5**			
	¼ yd.		Cut (2) 2" strips
■ **First Border**			
	1⅛ yds.		Cut (8) 4" strips
■ **Second Border**			
	1½ yds.		Cut (9) 5" strips
■ **Third Border**			
	2 yds.		Cut (10) 6" strips
Backing			
	6½ yds.		Cut (2) 3¼ yds. pieces
Batting			
	90" x 115"		
Binding for Machine Quilted Finish Only			
	1⅛ yds.		Cut (10) 3" strips

Lattice and Cornerstones

☐ **Fabric 1**			
Background	2⅝ yds.		Cut (8) 5" strips
			(8) 3½" strips
			(8) 2" strips
■ **Fabric 2**			
	1⅝ yds.		Cut (24) 2" strips
■ **Fabric 3**			
	1⅛ yds.		Cut (16) 2" strips
■ **Fabric 4**			
	⅔ yd.		Cut (8) 2" strips
■ **Fabric 5**			
	¼ yd.		Cut (2) 2" strips
■ **Lattice**			
	1¾ yds.		Cut (28) 2" strips
■ **Cornerstones**			
	⅓ yd.		Cut (3) 2" strips
■ **First Border**			
	1⅛ yds.		Cut (8) 4" strips
■ **Second Border**			
	1½ yds.		Cut (9) 5" strips
■ **Third Border**			
	2 yds.		Cut (10) 6" strips
Backing			
	6½ yds.		Cut (2) 3¼ yds. pieces
Batting			
	90" x 115"		
Binding for Machine Quilted Finish Only			
	1⅛ yds.		Cut (10) 3" strips

King Quilt

42 Blocks - 6 x 7   Approximate size: 96" x 107"
Cut all strips selvage to selvage.

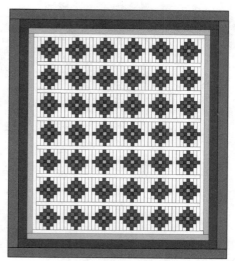
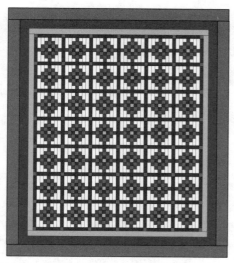

Classic

☐ **Fabric 1**		
Background	5 yds.	Cut (10) 5" strips
		(10) 3½" strips
		(42) 2" strips
■ **Fabric 2**		
	2 yds.	Cut (30) 2" strips
■ **Fabric 3**		
	1⅜ yds.	Cut (20) 2" strips
■ **Fabric 4**		
	⅞ yd.	Cut (10) 2" strips
■ **Fabric 5**		
	⅜ yd.	Cut (3) 2" strips
■ **First Border**		
	1¼ yds.	Cut (9) 4" strips
■ **Second Border**		
	1½ yds.	Cut (9) 5" strips
■ **Third Border**		
	2 yds.	Cut (10) 6" strips
Backing		
	9¾ yds.	Cut (3) 3¼ yds. pieces
Batting		
	108" x 115"	
Binding for Machine Quilted Finish Only		
	1⅛ yds.	Cut (11) 3" strips

Lattice and Cornerstones

☐ **Fabric 1**		
Background	3¼ yds.	Cut (10) 5" strips
		(10) 3½" strips
		(10) 2" strips
■ **Fabric 2**		
	2 yds.	Cut (30) 2" strips
■ **Fabric 3**		
	1⅜ yds.	Cut (20) 2" strips
■ **Fabric 4**		
	⅞ yd.	Cut (10) 2" strips
▨ **Fabric 5**		
	⅜ yd.	Cut (3) 2" strips
■ **Lattice**		
	2⅛ yds.	Cut (34) 2" strips
■ **Cornerstones**		
	⅓ yd.	Cut (3) 2" strips
▨ **First Border**		
	1¼ yds.	Cut (9) 4" strips
■ **Second Border**		
	1½ yds.	Cut (9) 5" strips
■ **Third Border**		
	2 yds.	Cut (10) 6" strips
Backing		
	9¾ yds.	Cut (3) 3¼ yds. pieces
Batting		
	108" x 115"	
Binding for Machine Quilted Finish Only		
	1⅛ yds.	Cut (11) 3" strips

Sewing Techniques

Sewing

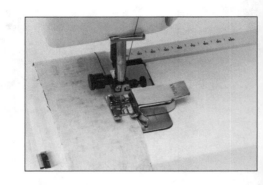

Stitch size

Use a small stitch, 12 to 15 to the inch or a setting of 2.

¼" seam allowance

It is important to use a consistent seam allowance throughout the entire construction. Typically fabric is fed under the presser foot at its right edge. This isn't necessarily a ¼". Make a test sample and measure the seam allowance. If necessary adjust the needle position, or change to a different presser foot, or feed the fabric under the presser foot to achieve the ¼". A magnetic seam guide placed at the right of the presser foot will assure a consistent seam allowance.

Conventional Seam

Serging

A person experienced with serging can construct the entire quilt with a serger. Or the strips can be serged and the resulting "section" pieces can be assembled on a conventional machine if the seam allowances are identical.

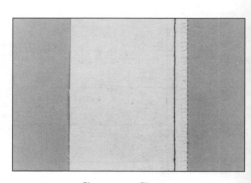

Serger Seam

Assembly-line sewing

This method saves time and thread by sewing a pair and butting on other pairs without cutting the thread until you are finished sewing. Assembly-line sewing isn't recommended with large or heavy pieces because the weight tends to cause pulling which results in crooked seams.

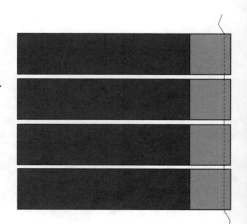

Pressing to "set and direct the seam allowance."

Throughout the construction, it is important to "set the seam" and then press the seam allowances in a given direction. To insure that the pieces have locking seams, do not use the common practice of pressing seams toward the darker side.

Strips or pairs of strips are sewn right sides together.

"Set the Seam"

Before opening, lay the sewn strips on the ironing board with a designated strip on the top. This top strip will always be a fabric **2** or **4** to insure that the block construction has locking seams. Lightly press the strips to "set the seam" as they lie right sides together.

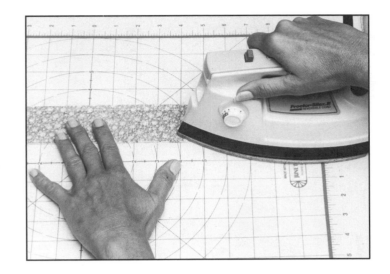

"Direct the Seam"

Lift the upper strip and press toward the fold. The seam will naturally fall behind the upper strip. Make sure there are no folds at the seam line.

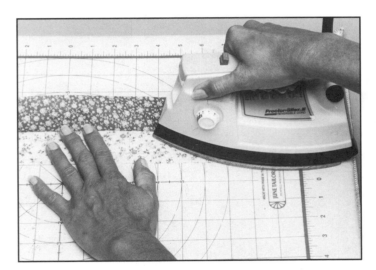

"Press Reverse Side"

Turn the strips over. Press the reverse side and check that the seams are pressed in the right direction.

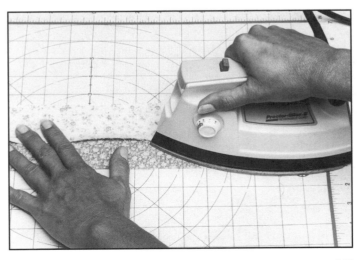

Making the Sections

The completed block consists of four different sections.

Sections A, B, and C are used twice. D, the center, is used once.

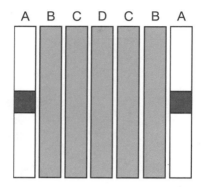

Making Section A

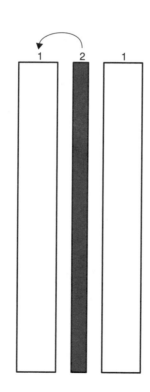

Count out these strips						
Use:	Baby	Lap	Twin	Double	Queen	King
5" wide strips of Fabric 1	2	4	4	8	8	10
2" wide strips of Fabric 2	1	2	2	4	4	5

Divide **1** into two equal stacks. Lay out with **2** in the middle.

1. Flip **2** right sides together to **1**. Sew the length of the strip using a ¼" seam allowance and 12-15 stitches per inch (or #2 on machine settings with 1-4). Clip threads.

2. If you are making a quilt larger than baby size, continue sewing additional pairs of **1** & **2** strips until all **2** strips and one stack of **1** strips are used. The second stack of **1** strips remain.

Pressing

Each time you are directed to "set and direct the seam" follow the instructions as shown in the Techniques Chapter. (Page 17.)

3. Lay strips on ironing board with **2** on top. "Set and direct the seam allowance" under **2**.

   Repeat pressing with remaining sewn strips.

4. Sew the remaining stacked **1** to the opposite side of **2** strip.

5. Lay strips on ironing board with **1** & **2** on top. "Set and direct the seam" under **2**.

   The wrong side, when pressed, will look like this.

   This completes construction of Section A. Label as A, and set aside.

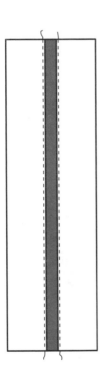

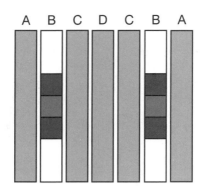

A B C D C B A

Making Section B

	Count out these strips					
Use:	**Baby**	**Lap**	**Twin**	**Double**	**Queen**	**King**
3 ½" wide strips of Fabric 1	2	4	4	8	8	10
2" wide strips of Fabric 2	2	4	4	8	8	10

Lay out strips in stacks.

1. Sew **2** to **1**.

2. Lay the strips on the ironing board with **2** on top. "Set and direct the seam" under **2**.

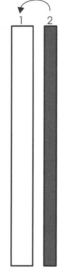

	Count out these strips					
Use:	**Baby**	**Lap**	**Twin**	**Double**	**Queen**	**King**
2" wide strips of Fabric 3	1	2	2	4	4	5

Divide the **1** and **2** pairs into two equal stacks. Lay out with **3** in the middle.

1. Sew **3** to **2** on one side.

2. Lay strips on ironing board with **1** & **2** on top. "Set and direct the seam" under **2**.

3. Sew remaining **2** & **1** to opposite side of **3**.

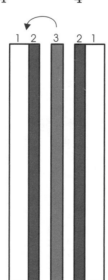

4. Lay strips on ironing board with pair **1** & **2** on top. "Set and direct the seam" under **2**.

The wrong side, when pressed, will look like this.

Label as B and set aside.

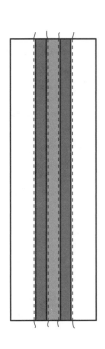

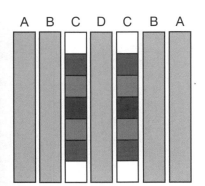

Making Section C

Count out these strips

Use:	Baby	Lap	Twin	Double	Queen	King
2" wide strips of Fabric 1	2	4	4	8	8	10
2" wide strips of Fabric 2	2	4	4	8	8	10

Lay out stacks of strips.

1. Sew **2** to **1**.

2. Lay the strips on the ironing board with **2** on top. "Set and direct the seam" under **2**.

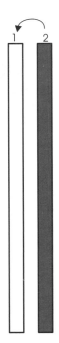

Use:	Baby	Lap	Twin	Double	Queen	King
2" wide strips of Fabric 3	2	4	4	8	8	10
2" wide strips of Fabric 4	1	2	2	4	4	5

Divide **3** into two equal stacks. Lay out with **4** in the middle.

1. Sew **4** to **3** on one side.

2. Lay the strips on the ironing board with **4** on top. "Set and direct the seam" under **4**.

3. Add **3** to opposite side of **4**.

4. Lay the strips on the ironing board with pair **3 & 4** on top. "Set and direct the seam" under **4**.

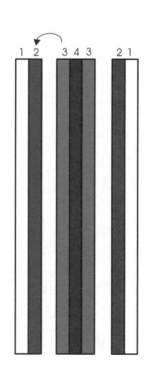

5. Divide the **1 & 2** pairs into two equal stacks. Lay out with **3 & 4 & 3** in the middle. Sew **3** to **2** on one side.

6. Lay strips on ironing board with **1 & 2** on top. "Set and direct the seam" under **2**.

7. Add remaining pairs of **2 & 1** to **3**.

8. Lay strips on ironing board with **1 & 2** on top. "Set and direct the seam" under **2**.

The wrong side when pressed will look like this.

Label as C and set aside.

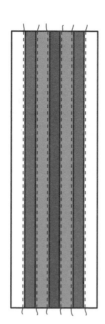

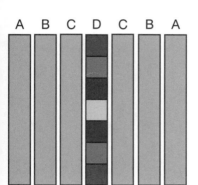

Making Section D

Count out these strips

Use:	Baby	Lap	Twin	Double	Queen	King
2" wide strips of Fabric 2	2	2	2	4	4	5
2" wide strips of Fabric 3	2	2	2	4	4	5

Lay out stacks of strips.

1. Sew **3** to **2**.

2. Lay strips on ironing board with **2** on top. "Set and direct the seam" under **2**.

King only: Cut one pair in half.

Use:	Baby	Lap	Twin	Double	Queen	King
2" wide strips of Fabric 4	2	2	2	4	4	5
2" wide strips of Fabric 5	1	1	1	2	2	3

Divide **4** into two equal stacks. Lay out with **5** in the middle.

King only: Cut one **4** in half and stack. Cut one **5** in half. Use one half and put one half aside.

1. Sew **5** to **4** on one side.

2. Lay the strips on the ironing board with **4** on top. "Set and direct the seam" under **4**.

3. Add the remaining **4** to the opposite side of **4** & **5**.

4. Lay strips on ironing board with **4** on the top. "Set and direct the seam" under **4**.

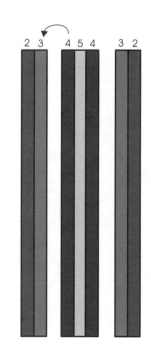

5. Divide pairs **2** & **3** into two equal stacks. Lay out with **4** & **5** & **4** in the middle. Add **4** to **3** on one side.

6. Lay strips on ironing board with **4** & **5** & **4** on top. "Set and direct the seam" under **4**.

7. Sew **3** & **2** to **4** on the opposite side.

8. Lay strips on ironing board with **2** & **3** & **4** & **5** & **4** on top. "Set and direct the seam" under **4**.

The wrong side, when pressed, will look like this.

Label as D and set aside.

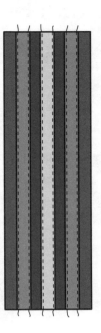

Cutting and Sewing the Sections into Blocks

Sections A and B

1. With Section B on top, place right sides together with Section A. Lay on ironing board carefully matching seams. The widths of the sections may not be the same. Press the length of the pair to help lock the seams.

2. Position the layered Sections on gridded cutting mat, lining up bottom edge with grid line. Square left edge of sections to straighten, and remove selvage.

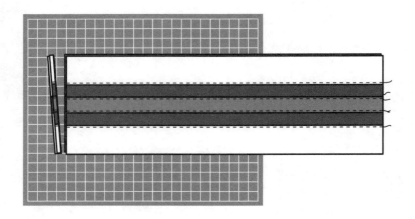

Number of layered pairs to cut for your size quilt

Baby	Lap	Twin	Double	Queen	King
18	36	36	70	70	84

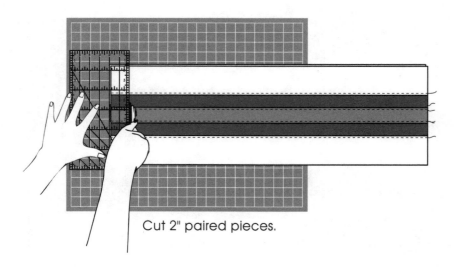

Cut 2" paired pieces.

3. Cut 2" wide layered pairs. Stack pairs in piles of 10 for easy counting.

Hints to keep in mind:

Always match seams.

Do not try to ease or pinch the Section A to match at the ends of Section B; any excess will be trimmed off later.

If you are an inexperienced sewer, you may want to pin each seam, and remove the pin just before you reach it while sewing.

A stiletto is helpful to hold a seam in place while sewing.

1. Match the seams. With B on top, right sides together with A, sew the length of the pair. Do not remove from machine. Assembly-line sew by butting on new pairs. Check to see that seams match and lock.

2. Clip threads and stack.

3. Lay a pair on the ironing board with section B on top. "Set and direct the seam" under B. Repeat with remaining pairs.

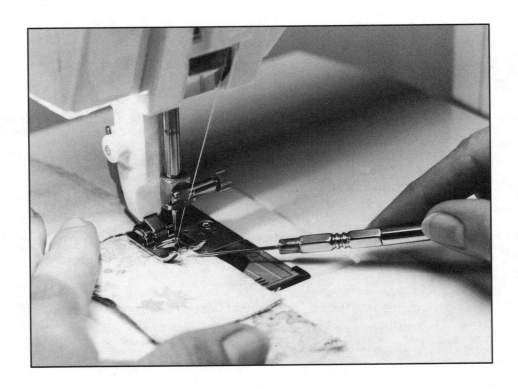

Sections C and D

1. With Section D on top, place right sides together with Section C. Carefully line up seams. Press the length of the pair.

2. Position on gridded cutting mat. Square left side to straighten edges and remove selvages.

3. Cut 2" wide layered pairs.

Number of layered pairs to cut for your size quilt

Baby	Lap	Twin	Double	Queen	King
9	18	18	35	35	42

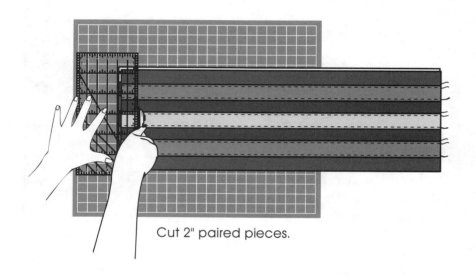

Cut 2" paired pieces.

Cutting and stacking additional C segments

Baby Remove section D and discard. Continue cutting 9 additional C segments. Stack.

Lap or twin From a Section C cut 18 more segments. Stack.

Double, queen For convenient cutting, layer two C sections together, right sides up on cutting mat. Square left side. Cut 35 C segments. Stack.

King For convenient cutting, layer two C sections together, right sides up on cutting mat. Square left side. Cut 42 segments. Stack.

4. Sew the paired C and D segments, matching seams.

5. Lay pair on ironing board with D on top. "Set and direct the seam" under D.

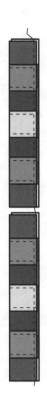

6. Sew remaining stacked C to opposite side of C/D.

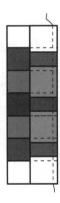

7. Lay on ironing board with C/D on top. "Set and direct the seam" under D.

8. Divide pairs A/B into two equal stacks with C/D/C stack in the middle.

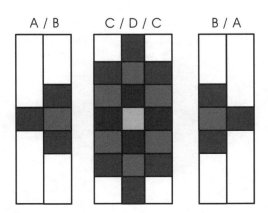

A / B   C / D / C   B / A

9. Sew C to B.

10. Lay on ironing board with A/B on top. "Set the seam" under B.

11. Sew remaining B to opposite side of C.

12. Lay on ironing board with A /B on top. "Set the seam" under B.

The wrong side when pressed will look like this.

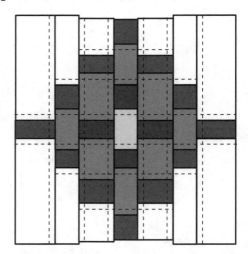

This completes the construction of the block.

Count your blocks.

Squaring the Blocks

The blocks will likely have uneven edges due to the number of seams in the different sections. The uneven edges will be trimmed while centering the Square Up ruler on the block.

Finding the Average Size of Your Blocks

Ideally the blocks are 11" square, but probably will be smaller. Use a 12 ½" Square Up ruler to measure several blocks to find the average size. Position the Square Up ruler with its 6" lines on the left and bottom seams of the block's center square.

The ruler's diagonal line should cross that square from corner to corner. Look along the top and right edges of the ruler.

If the number **2** fabric comes to the ruler edges and to the ruler's 10 ½" squaring lines, this is a 10 ½ " square block.

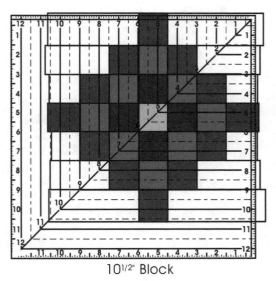

10¹⁄₂" Block

If the block is generally shy of 10 ½", move the ruler so that its 6" lines are ⅛" to the left and below the seams of the center square. This results in a 10 ¼" square block.

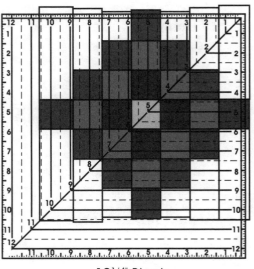

10¹⁄₄" Block

31

If the block is generally larger than 10 ½", move the ruler so that its 6" lines are ⅛" to the right and above those seams of the center square. This results in a 10 ¾" square block.

Measure several blocks and then circle your average measurement

10 ¼"   10 ½"   10 ¾"   11"

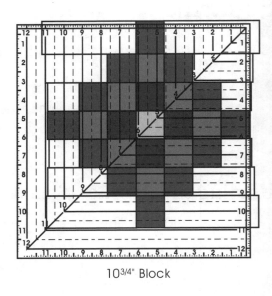

10¾" Block

Trimming to Square the Block Evenly

It is important to trim evenly. Trimming excess from only two sides would result in an off-center block.

Trim all blocks to the same size. Be careful to align ruler lines on or parallel with seams to keep the block square and the pattern centered.

1. Position the ruler for your average size block.

2. Rotary cut along the right and top edge to remove excess fabric and square two sides of the block.

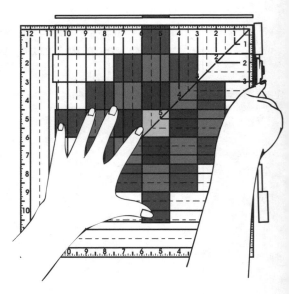

3. Give the block a half turn. Reposition ruler exactly as for the first cut. Trim the remaining sides.

4. Measure block to confirm recorded measurement.

5. Repeat for all blocks.

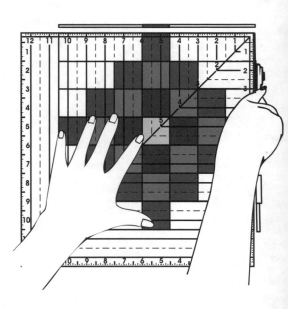

Setting the Top Together

The Bird's Eye blocks are set together with strips of the same background fabric for a Classic Bird's Eye Quilt, or they are set together with Lattice and Cornerstones. See page 40 for the Lattice and Cornerstone setting.

Classic Bird's Eye Setting

Adding the Vertical Strips of Background Fabric

Count out these strips

Use:	Baby	Lap	Twin	Double	Queen	King
2" wide strips of Fabric 1	2	4	4	10	10	12

1. Stack and lay on cutting mat. Square the ends, cutting off selvage.

2. Refer to your recorded measurement of squared block. Cut and stack vertical pieces that length. You will get either 3 or 4 pieces per strip.

Cut this many vertical pieces

Use:	Baby	Lap	Twin	Double	Queen	King
2" wide strips of Fabric 1	6	12	12	28	28	35

3. Stack the same number of blocks, with Section A next to the stack of vertical strips. Make sure the **1** fabric seams of the blocks are vertical. **You will not add vertical strips to all blocks at this step.**

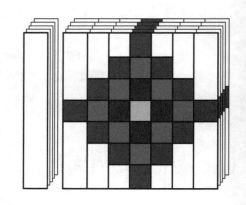

4. Flip block onto strip, right sides together. Pin ends to match. Sew the length easing or stretching to fit. Repeat with all strips.

5. Lay block on ironing board with strip on top. "Set and direct the seam." **Seam allowance will always be pressed under the strip**.

6. Divide the blocks, with vertical strips, into 2 equal stacks.

   King only: Put 14 into each stack and set extras aside for later.

7. Right side up, lay block on flat surface. Line up the ruler with the edge of the strip and a seam. Back off the ruler enough to mark a short pencil line in the seam allowance of the strip to line up with seam. Repeat with remaining seams.

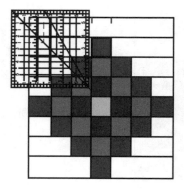

8. Flip the blocks right sides together. Pin match at the seams. Pin block to strip at edge. Pin ends to match. Sew the length of the block, easing or stretching. Repeat for all pairs.

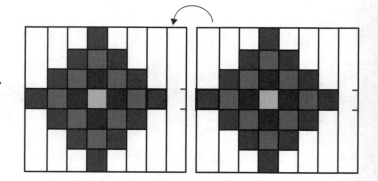

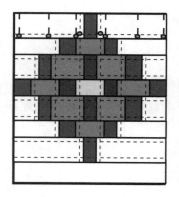

9. Lay pair of blocks on ironing board with strip on top. "Set and direct the seam."

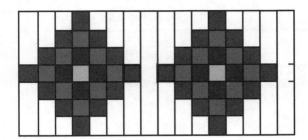

10. **Baby, lap and twin:** These units are done. Go on to step 14.

11. **Double, queen and king:** Divide pairs of blocks into two stacks. Repeat step 8. Each unit will now be 4 blocks wide.

12. Lay unit on ironing board with strip on top. "Set and direct the seam."

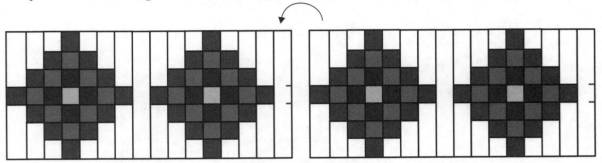

13. **King only:** Repeat step 8, adding remaining single blocks to strip sides. Lay unit on ironing board with strip on top. "Set and direct the seam."

14. **All sizes:** Sew remaining single blocks to strip side of each block unit. No unit will end in a strip.

15. Lay unit on ironing board with strip on top. "Set and direct the seam."

16. Each unit is a row.

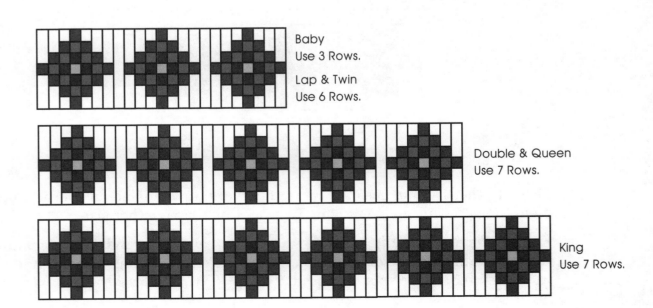

Baby
Use 3 Rows.

Lap & Twin
Use 6 Rows.

Double & Queen
Use 7 Rows.

King
Use 7 Rows.

Adding the Horizontal Strips of Background Fabric

	Baby	Lap	Twin	Double	Queen	King
Count out these strips						
Use:						
2" wide strips of Fabric 1	2	5	5	9	9	12

1. Stack and lay on cutting mat. Square the ends, cutting off the selvage.

2. **Baby, lap, twin:** Use single strips.

   Double, queen: Cut 3 strips in half. Sew these (6) half strips to the (6) full strips.

   King: Sew the (12) strips into (6) pairs.

   Lay out the rows with the strips between them.

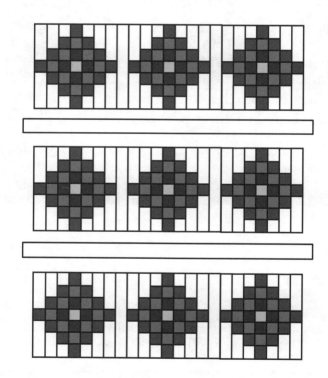

3. Measure the length across the center of several rows to find an average measurement. Record your measurement _____. Cut strips to that size.

4. Right sides together, flip a row down onto a strip. Match and pin the middle of the strip to the middle of the bottom edge of the row. Pin at the ends and midway as necessary for your size quilt.

5. Sew, easing or stretching. Repeat for each strip. There will be one row of blocks without a strip attached for each size quilt.

6. With strip on top, lay on ironing board. "Set and direct the seam."

7. Right side up, lay row with attached strip on flat surface. Starting at the right end, line up the ruler with the edge of the strip and first seam. Back off the ruler enough to mark a short pencil line in the seam allowance of the strip to line up with the seam.

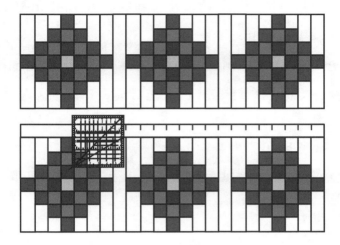

8. Repeat on all seams of that row and remaining rows.

9. Flip two rows together. Pin at ends and pin match the marks with the seams.

10. Sew length of the row easing or stretching between pins. Remove pins as you come to them. Check for accuracy in matching when done. Correct any mismatches.

11. "Set and direct the seam" as you go.

12. There should be no strip around the entire setting.

Framing the Entire Classic Bird's Eye Quilt Top

Use:	Baby	Lap	Twin	Double	Queen	King
2" wide strips of Fabric 1	4	6	6	7	7	8

1. Stack and lay on cutting mat. Square ends of strips, cutting off selvage.

2. **Baby:** Use (4) single strips.

   Lap, twin: Sew (4) strips into (2) pairs. Use (2) single strips.

   Double, queen: Cut (1) strip in half and sew these to (2) full strips. Sew (4) strips into (2) pairs.

   King: Sew (8) strips into (4) pairs.

3. Measure the length along the middle of quilt. Cut strips for the sides at this measurement.

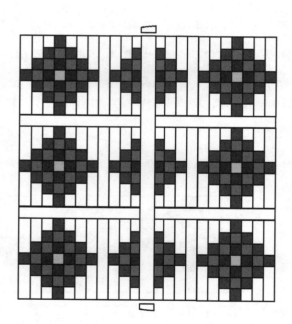

4. With block side on top, right sides together, pin the middle of the strips to the middle of the sides. Pin at the ends and midway as necessary for your size quilt.

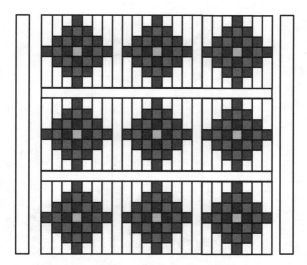

5. Sew the length, easing or stretching to fit.

6. With strip on top, place on ironing board. "Set and direct the seams" for both sides of quilt.

7. Measure the width along the middle of the quilt. Cut strips for the top and bottom at this measurement.

8. With block side on top, right sides together, pin the middle of the strips to the middle of the top and bottom. Pin at the ends and midway as necessary for your size quilt.

9. Sew, easing or stretching to fit.

10. With strip on top, place on ironing board. "Set and direct the seams" for the top and bottom sides of the quilt.

Lattice and Cornerstone Setting

Adding the Vertical Lattice Strips

	Count out these strips					
Use:	Baby	Lap	Twin	Double	Queen	King
2" wide strips of Fabric 6	4	8	8	14	14	17

1. Stack and lay on gridded cutting mat. Square the ends, cutting off the selvage.

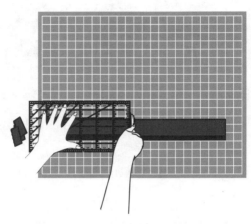

2. Refer to your recorded measurement for squared block and cut pieces that length. You will get either 3 or 4 lattice pieces per strip.

	Cut this many lattice pieces					
Use:	Baby	Lap	Twin	Double	Queen	King
2" wide strips of Fabric 6	12	24	24	42	42	49

3. Stack all blocks with Section A next to the stack of lattice. Make sure the **1** fabric seams in the blocks are vertical.

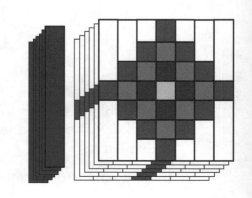

4. Flip block right sides together with lattice. Pin ends to match and sew the length. Repeat until all blocks are used.

5. Add remaining stacked lattice to opposite side, resulting in some blocks having two vertical lattice strips.

6. With lattice on top, place on ironing board. "Set and direct the seams." **The seam allowance will always be under the lattice.**

7. For all sizes but King, set aside the two lattice-sided blocks.

8. Divide remaining blocks into two equal stacks.

King only: Place two lattice-sided blocks in one of the stacks.

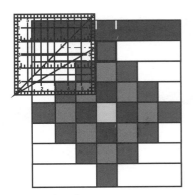

9. Right side up, lay block on flat surface. Line up the ruler with the edge of the strip and a seam. Back off the ruler enough to mark a short pencil line in the seam allowance of the strip to line up with seam. Repeat with remaining seam.

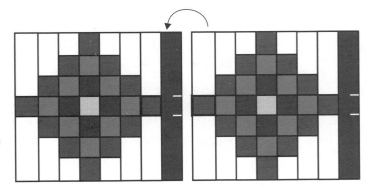

10. Flip the blocks right sides together. Pin match at the seams. Pin block to lattice along edge. Pin ends to match. Sew the length of the block, easing or stretching to fit. Repeat for all pairs.

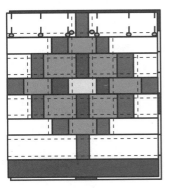

11. Lay pair of blocks on ironing board with lattice on top. "Set and direct the seam."

12. Stack the pairs.

Baby, lap, twin: These units are done. Go on to step 14.

Double, queen: Divide pairs of blocks into two equal stacks. Repeat step 10 to make units of four blocks.

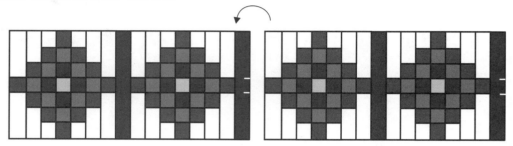

King: Set aside the pairs of blocks with the extra lattice strips. Divide 14 pairs of blocks into two equal stacks. Repeat step 10 to make rows of four blocks.

13. With lattice on top, place on ironing board. "Set and direct the seam."

14. Add a remaining block to each row.

15. With lattice on top, place on ironing board. "Set and direct the seam."

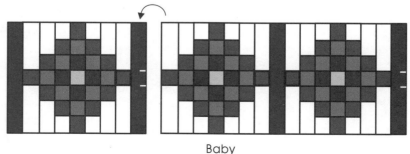

Baby

Preparing the Horizontal Lattice

	Count out these strips					
Use:	Baby	Lap	Twin	Double	Queen	King
2" wide strips of Fabric 6	4	7	7	14	14	17

1. Stack and lay on cutting mat. Square the left edge, cutting off the selvage.

2. Refer to your recorded block measurement and cut pieces that length. You will get either 3 or 4 lattice pieces per strip.

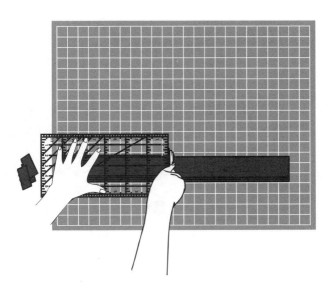

	Cut this many lattice pieces					
Use:	Baby	Lap	Twin	Double	Queen	King
2" wide strips of Fabric 6	12	21	21	40	40	48

Preparing the Cornerstones

Use:	Baby	Lap	Twin	Double	Queen	King
2" wide strips of Fabric 7	1	2	2	3	3	3

Lay on cutting mat. Square the left edge, cutting off the selvage.

Cut and stack 2" square cornerstone pieces.

Cut this many cornerstones

Use:	Baby	Lap	Twin	Double	Queen	King
2" wide strips of Fabric 7	16	28	28	48	48	56

Sewing Strips of Horizontal Lattice and Cornerstones

1. Assembly-line sew your number of lattice strips to cornerstones. Set aside remaining cornerstones.

2. With lattice on top, place on ironing board. **"Set and direct the seams under the lattice"** for all sewn pieces.

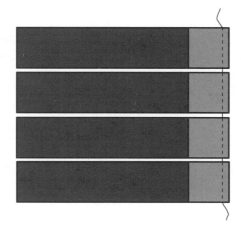

3. Lay out stacks for your quilt size:

   Baby: Divide lattice/cornerstone strips into four equal stacks with 3 in each.

   Lap, twin: Divide lattice/cornerstone strips into seven equal stacks with 3 in each.

   Double, queen: Divide lattice/cornerstone strips into eight equal stacks with 5 in each.

   King: Divide lattice and cornerstone strips into eight equal stacks with 6 in each.

4. Using two pairs from the first stack, stitch cornerstone to lattice. Repeat for all stacks.

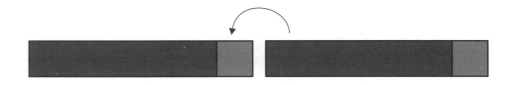

5. With lattice on top, place on ironing board. "Set and direct the seam."

6. Continue butting on one pair to each row until all lattice are used. "Set and direct the seam" after each addition.

7. Add remaining cornerstone to lattice. "Set and direct the seam."

Adding the Lattice/Cornerstone Strips to the Block Rows

1. With block side on top, put right sides together with lattice. Match and pin each cornerstone to lattice end across the length. Pin at intervals. Stitch the length.

2. Repeat until each row of blocks has a lattice/cornerstone strip. Add remaining lattice/cornerstone strip to top row.

3. With lattice on top, place on ironing board. "Set and direct the seams."

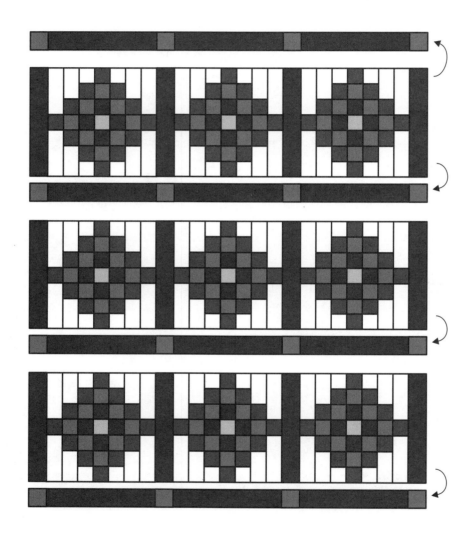

Sewing the Rows Together

1. Lay out the rows.

2. Starting at the right end of the second row line up the ruler with edge of the lattice and the seam of the block. Back off the ruler enough to mark a short pencil line in the seam allowance of the strip to line up with the seam.

3. Repeat on all seams of that row.

4. Flip two rows together. Pin at ends and cornerstone seams. Pin match the marks with seams.

5. Sew the length of the row easing or stretching between pins. Remove pins as you come to them. Check for accuracy in matching when done. Correct any mismatches.

6. "Set and direct the seam" as you go.

Adding the Borders

Designing Your Borders

Be creative when adding borders. Suggested border yardage and border examples are given for each quilt. However, you may wish to custom design the borders by changing the widths of the strips. This might change backing and batting yardage.

When custom fitting the quilt, lay the top on your bed before adding the borders and backing. Measure to find how much border is needed to get the fit you want. Keep in mind that the quilt will "shrink" approximately 3" in the length and width after tying, "stitching in the ditch," and/or machine quilting.

Piecing Borders and Optional Binding Strips

1. Stack and square off the ends of each strip, trimming away the selvage edges.

2. Seam the strips of each fabric into long pieces by assembly-line sewing. Lay the first strip right side up. Lay the second strip right sides to it. Backstitch, stitch the short ends together, and backstitch again.

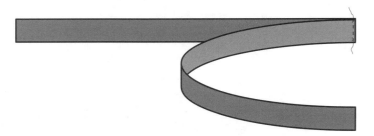

3. Take the strip on the top and fold it so the right side is up.

4. Place the third strip right sides to it, backstitch, stitch, and backstitch again.

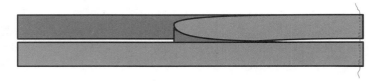

5. Continue assembly-line sewing all the short ends together into long pieces for each fabric.

6. Clip the threads holding the strips together.

7. Press seams to one side.

Sewing the Borders to the Quilt Top

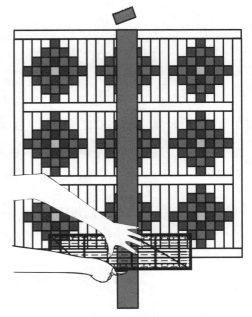

1. Measure down the center to find the length. Cut two side strips that measurement **plus two inchs.**

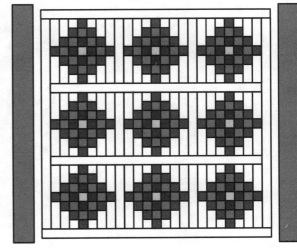

2. Right sides together, match and pin the center of the strips to the center of the sides. Pin at ends, allowing an extra inch of border at each end. Pin intermittently. Sew with the quilt on top. "Set and direct the seams," pressing toward the borders.

3. Square the ends even with the top and bottom of the quilt.

4. Measure the width across the center including newly added borders. Cut two strips that measurement plus two inchs.

5. Right sides together, match and pin the center of the strips to the center of the top and bottom edges of the quilt. Pin at the ends, allowing an extra inch of border at both ends. Pin intermittently. Sew with the quilt on top.

6. "Set and direct the seams," pressing toward the borders. Square the ends even with the side borders.

   Repeat these steps for additional borders.

Finishing: Machine Quilting with Binding Option

The options are Machine Quilting with a Binding or a Quick Turn and Tie. Quick Turn and Tie is the easier method found on page 58.

Machine Quilting with a Binding Finish

Use a thin batting for machine quilting. The layers are pinned with #1 safety pins. A walking foot attachment for the sewing machine feeds the three layers evenly. Invisible thread on the top and a regular bobbin thread to match the backing holds the quilt layers together and offers an attractive finish.

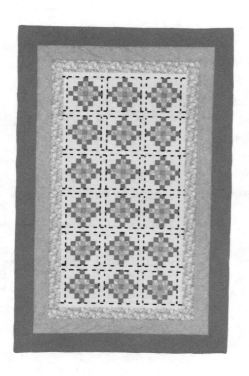
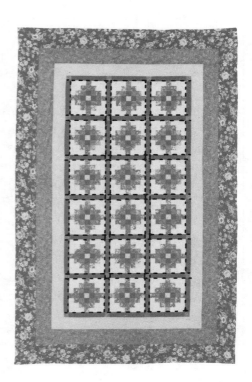

Marking the Quilt Top

You may mark the quilt after stretching it out and clamping or taping it down, or you may wait until it is layered. Decide where you want the quilting lines. With the 6" x 24" ruler, lightly mark the lines for machine quilting. Use chalk, a thin dry sliver of soap, a hera tool, or a silver pencil. Make certain that you can remove the marks from the fabric.

Layering Quilt Top with Backing and Batting

1. Piece the backing yardage together for larger size quilts.

2. Stretch out the backing right side down on a large floor area or table. Tape down on a floor area or clamp onto a table with large binder clips.

3. Place and smooth out the batting on top. Lay the quilt top right side up and centered on top of the batting. Completely smooth and stretch all layers until they are flat. Tape or clip securely. The backing and batting should extend at least 2" on all sides.

4. Mark the quilting lines if this hasn't been done.

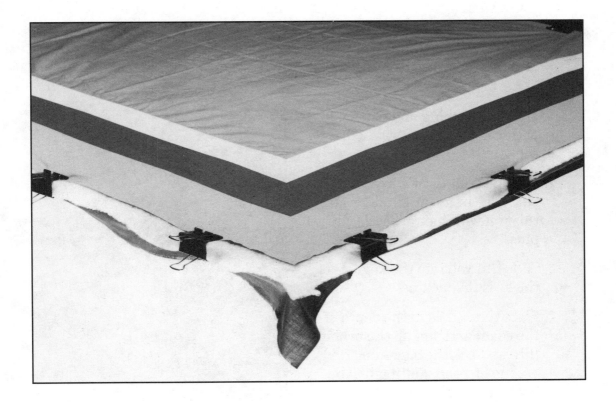

Quick and Easy Safety Pinning

Place safety pins throughout the quilt away from the marked quilting lines. Begin pinning in the center and work to the outside, spacing them every 5".

Grasp the opened pin in your right hand and the pinning tool in your left hand. Push the pin through the three layers, and bring the tip of the pin back out. Catch the tip in the groove of the tool and allow point to extend far enough to push pin closure down.

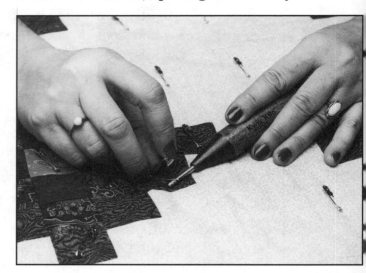

Machine Quilting the Marked Lines

Use a walking foot attachment for straight line quilting. Use invisible thread in the top of your machine and regular thread in the bobbin to match the backing. Loosen the top tension, and lengthen your stitch to 8 - 10 stitches per inch, or a #3 or #4 setting. Free arm machines need the "bed" placed for more surface area.

1. Trim the backing and batting to within 2" of the outside edge of the quilt.

2. Roll the quilt tightly from the outside edge in toward middle. Hold this roll with metal bicycle clips or pins.

3. Slide this roll into the keyhole of the sewing machine.

4. Place the needle in the depth of the seam and pull up the bobbin thread. Lock the beginning and ending of each quilting line by backstitching ½".

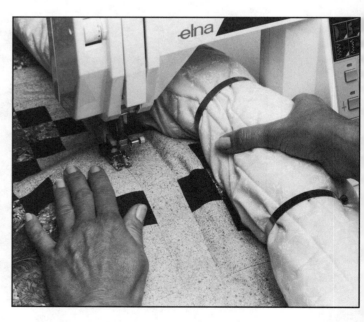

5. Place your hands flat on both sides of the needle to form a hoop. Keep the quilt area flat and tight. If you need to ease in the top fabric, feed the quilt through the machine by pushing the layers of fabric and batting forward underneath the walking foot.

6. If puckering occurs, remove stitching by grasping the bobbin thread with a pin or tweezers and pull gently to expose the invisible thread. Touch the invisible thread stitches with the rotary cutter blade as you pull the bobbin thread free from the quilt.

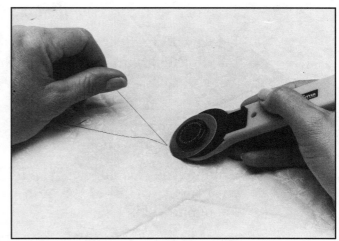

7. Unroll, roll, and machine quilt on all lines, sewing the length or width or diagonal of the quilt.

Adding the Binding

See page 48 for piecing the binding strips.

Use a walking foot attachment and regular thread on top and in the bobbin to match the binding. Use 10 stitches per inch, or #3 setting.

1. Press the binding strip in half lengthwise with right sides out.

2. Line up the raw edges of the folded binding with the raw edge of the quilt top at the middle of one side.

3. Begin sewing 4" from the end of the binding.

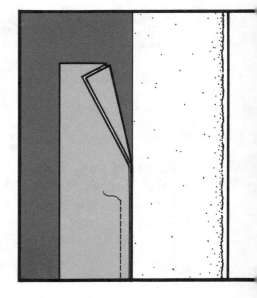

4. At the corner, stop the stitching ¼" from the edge with the needle in the fabric. Raise the presser foot and turn the quilt to the next side. Put the foot back down.

5. Sew backwards ¼" to the edge of the binding, raise the foot, and pull the quilt forward slightly.

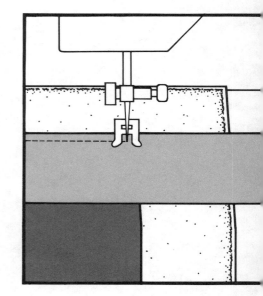

6. Fold the binding strip straight up on the diagonal. Fingerpress in the diagonal fold.

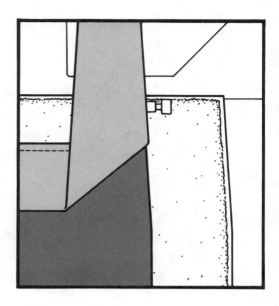

7. Fold the binding strip straight down with the diagonal fold underneath. Line up the top of the fold with the raw edge of the binding underneath.

8. Begin sewing from the corner.

9. Continue sewing and mitering the corners around the outside of the quilt.

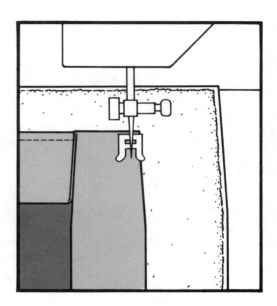

10. Stop sewing 4" from where the ends will over-lap.

11. Line up the two ends of binding. Trim the excess with a ½" overlap. Open out the folded ends and pin right sides together. Sew a ¼" seam.

12. Continue to sew the binding in place.

13. Trim the batting and backing up to the raw edges of the binding.

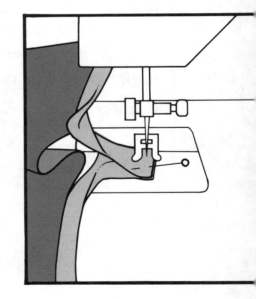

14. Fold the binding to the backside of the quilt. Pin in place so that the folded edge on the binding covers the stitching line. Tuck in the excess fabric at each miter on the diagonal.

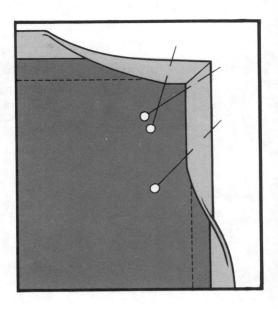

15. From the right side, "stitch in the ditch" using invisible thread on the right side, and a bobbin thread to match the binding on the back side. Catch the folded edge of the binding on the back side with the stitching.

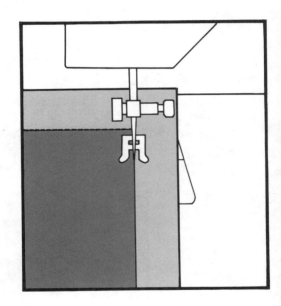

Finishing: Quick Turn and Tie Option

The Quick Turn method is the easier and faster way of finishing the quilt. Thick batting is "rolled" into the middle of the quilt, and the layers are held together with ties of embroidery floss. Borders may be "stitched in the ditch" for additional dimension. For this stitching, use a walking foot sewing machine attachment to keep the layers feeding evenly. Use invisible thread in the top and a regular bobbin thread to match the backing.

Sewing and Layering a Quick Turn

1. Piece backing yardage together for larger size quilts.

2. Lay out the oversized backing fabric, right side up, on a large table or floor. Clamp to the table with binder clips or tape to the floor.

3. Lay the quilt top on the backing fabric with right sides together. Stretch and smooth the top. Pin. Trim away excess backing. They should be the same size.

4. Use a ¼" seam allowance and sew around the four sides of the quilt, leaving a 24" opening in the middle of one long side. Do not turn the quilt right side out.

5. Lay the quilt on top of the batting. Smooth and trim the batting to the same size as the quilt top.

6. To assure that the batting stays out to the edges, whipstitch the batting to the ¼" seam allowance around the outside edge of the quilt.

Turning the Quilt Top

One person can turn the quilt alone, but it's helpful if two or three others can help. Read this whole section before beginning.

1. If you are working with a group, station the people at the corners of the quilt. If working alone, start in one corner opposite the opening.

2. Roll the corners and sides tightly to keep the batting in place as you roll toward the opening.

   If several people are helping, all should roll toward the opening. If only one is doing the rolling, use a knee to hold down one corner while stretching over to the other corners.

3. Open up the opening over this huge wad of fabric and batting, and pop the quilt right side out through the hole.

4. Unroll carefully with the layers together.

5. Lay the quilt flat on the floor or on a very large table. Work out all wrinkles and bumps by stationing two people opposite each other around the quilt. Have each person grasp the edge and tug the quilt in opposite directions.

6. You can also relocate any batting by reaching inside the quilt through the opening with a yardstick. Hold the edges and shake the batting into place if necessary.

7. Slipstitch the opening shut.

Finishing the Quick Turn Quilt

You may choose to tie your entire quilt, or machine quilt by "stitching in the ditch" around the borders and tying in the blocks. A quilt with thick batting is difficult to machine quilt because it is hard to get all the rolled thickness to fit through the keyhole of the sewing machine. You can, however, machine quilt by "stitching in the ditch" along the border seams.

Tying the Quilt

1. Thread a large-eyed curved needle with six strands of embroidery floss, crochet thread, or other thread of your choice.

2. Plan where you want your ties placed, about 5 to 8 inches apart. Do not tie in the borders if you wish to "stitch in the ditch."

3. Starting in the center of the quilt and working to the outside, take a ¼" stitch through all thicknesses at the points you wish to tie. Draw the curved needle along to each point, going in and out, and replacing the tying material as needed.

4. Clip all the stitches midway.

5. Tie the strands into surgeon's square knots by taking the strand on the right and wrapping it twice. Pull the knot tight. Take the strand on the left, wrap it twice, and pull the knot tight.

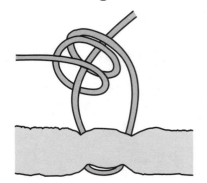
Right over left and wrap twice.

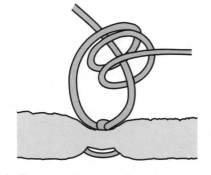
Left over right and wrap twice.

6. Clip the strands so they are ½" to 1" long.

Stitching in the Ditch

For more dimensional borders, you many choose to "stitch in the ditch" rather than tie the borders. A walking foot or even-feed foot sewing machine attachment is necessary to keep the three layers feeding at the same rate.

1. Change your stitch length to 10 stitches per inch or #3 setting. Match your bobbin color of thread to your backing color. Loosen the top tension and thread with the soft nylon invisible thread.

2. Safety pin the length of the borders. See page 52 for pinning instructions.

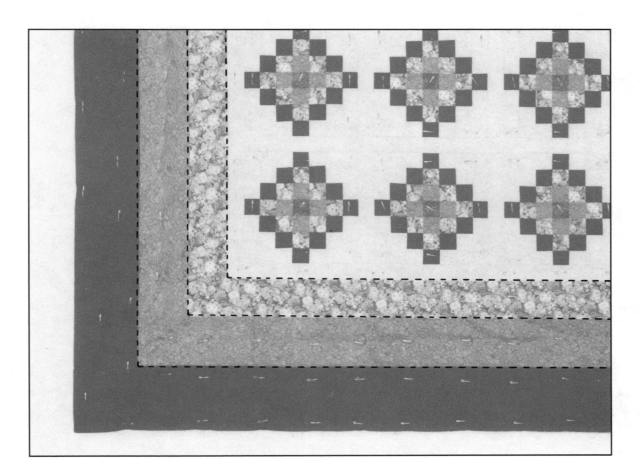

3. Place the needle in the depth of the seam and pull up the bobbin thread. Lock the beginning and ending of the quilting line by backstitching ½". Run your hand underneath to feel for puckers. Grasp the quilt with your left hand above the sewing machine, and grasp the quilt ten inches below the walking foot with your right hand as you stitch. If you need to ease in the top fabric, feed the quilt through the machine by pushing the layers of fabric and batting forward underneath the walking foot.

If puckering occurs, remove stitching by grasping the bobbin thread with a pin or tweezers and pull gently to expose the invisible thread. Touch the invisible thread stitches with the rotary cutter blade as you pull the bobbin thread free from the quilt. See page 53 for removing invisible stitches.

Index

rder Information

ou do not have a quilt shop in your area, you may write for a complete catalog and current price list of all
ks and patterns published by Quilt in a Day®, Inc.

ks

lt in a Day Log Cabin
Sampler--A Machine Sewn Quilt
of Treasured Quilts
er's Knot Quilt
ish Quilt in a Day
h Chain in a Day
ntry Christmas
nies and Blossoms
y Basket Quilt
mond Log Cabin Tablecloth or Treeskirt
rning Star Quilt
Around the World Quilt
endship Quilt
sden Plate Quilt, A Simplified Method
eapple Quilt, a Piece of Cake
liant Star Quilt
zing Star Tablecloth
ip Quilt
ap Quilt, Strips and Spider Webs
rgoyne Surrounded
abonnet Sue Visits Quilt in a Day
d's Eye
ating With Color
ck Party Series 1
Quilter's Year
ck Party Series 2
Baskets & Flowers
ck Party Series 3
Quilters Almanac
ck Party Series 4
Christmas Traditions

Booklets and Patterns

Patchwork Santa
Last Minute Gifts
Dresden Plate Placemats and Tea Cozy
Angel of Antiquity
Log Cabin Wreath Wallhanging
Log Cabin Christmas Tree Wallhanging
Flying Geese Quilt
Miniature May Basket Wallhanging
Tulip Table Runner and Wallhanging
Heart's Delight, Nine-Patch Variations
Country Flag Wallhanging
Spools and Tools Wallhanging
Schoolhouse Wallhanging
Star for all Seasons

Videos

Log Cabin Video
Lover's Knot Video
Irish Chain Video
Ohio Star Video
Blazing Star Video
Scrap Quilt Video
Morning Star Video
Trip Around the World Video
Pineapple Video
Radiant Star Video
Flying Geese Video
. . . . and many others

ou are ever in San Diego County, southern California, drop by the Quilt in a Day Center quilt shop and class-
m in the La Costa Meadows Business Park. Write ahead for a current class schedule and map.
anor Burns may be seen on Educational Public Broadcasting Stations (PBS) throughout the country. Check
r TV listing in your area for dates and times.

Quilt in a Day®, Inc.
1955 Diamond Street, San Marcos, California 92069
Phone: 1(800)825-9458 Information Line: 1(619)591-0929 FAX: 1(619)591-4424